CW00418280

WELSH WIT

quips and quotes

TOM HAY

summersdale

WELSH WIT

Summersdale Publishers Ltd
46 West Street
Chichester
West Sussex
PO19 1RP
UK

www.summersdale.com

Printed and bound in Singapore

ISBN: 978-1-84024-732-9

Disclaimer
Every effort has been made to attribute the quotations in this collection to the correct source. Should there be any omissions or errors in this respect we apologise and shall be pleased to make the appropriate acknowledgements in any future editions.

Contents

Editor's Note

The renowned poet Dannie Abse once remarked that, 'It's easier to quote someone than to think for oneself.' You'll find plenty of opportunities to do just that, and do it with style, in this hilarious compendium of the best one-liners Wales has to offer.

Though the Welsh are a talented bunch, they're not too proud to poke fun at themselves. Take, for example, Harry Secombe's explanation for why the Welsh are such good singers: because they 'have no locks on their bathroom doors'; or the legendary actor Richard Burton's comment on the dramatic inclinations of his fellow countrymen: 'The Welsh are all actors. It's only the bad ones who turn professional.'

From Tommy Cooper to Catherine Zeta Jones and Dylan Thomas to Shirley Bassey, there's certainly no shortage of celebrated characters who hail from the Land of Song, and they've got plenty to say about subjects as diverse as eating and drinking, love and marriage, politics and much more.

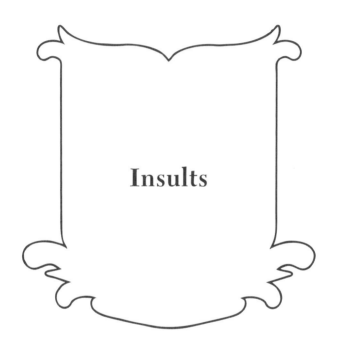

Insults

He's got a photographic mind. It's a pity it never developed.

Hywel Roberts

The English rugby team?
I've seen better centres in
a box of Black Magic.

Max Boyce

Arthur Balfour's impact on
history is no more than the whiff
of scent on a lady's handkerchief.

David Lloyd George

Muhammad Ali wouldn't have hit Joe Louis on the bum with a handful of rice.

Tommy Farr

If you took off your spectacles and sat on the fire, the room would be full of the smell of roast pork.

Dylan Thomas

She's the sort of woman who lives for others, and you can tell the others by their hunted expression.

C. S. Lewis

A beautiful doughnut covered in diamonds and paint.

Alan Williams on Elizabeth Taylor

If I was in the gutter, which I ain't, he'd still be looking up at me from the sewer.

Neil Kinnock on Michael Heseltine

*When I was born my mother
said I looked like a frog.*

Catherine Zeta Jones

*You were a weak, pale,
pusillanimous imitation
of Laurence Olivier.*

Meredith Jones to Richard Burton regarding
his *Henry V* performance

The right honourable gentleman has sat for so long on the fence that the iron has entered his soul.

David Lloyd George

Sport

I think you enjoy the game more if you don't know the rules. Anyway, you're on the same wavelength as the referees.

Jonathan Davies on rugby

If I had to make the choice between staying married and playing snooker, snooker would win.

Ray Reardon

We've lost seven of our last eight matches. Only team that we've beaten was Western Samoa. Good job we didn't play the whole of Samoa.

Gareth Davies

*Every time I hear the name Joe
Louis my nose starts to bleed.*

Tommy Farr

*It takes two hours to get
ready – hot bath, shave my
legs and face, moisturise, put
fake tan on and do my hair
– which takes a bit of time.*

Gavin Henson

I hope Barry Hearn doesn't go out of snooker because the only other job he would want is God's and that will take a bit of getting.

Cliff Wilson

Moving from Wales to Italy is like moving to a different country.

Ian Rush

Rugby is a wonderful show. Dance, opera and, suddenly, the blood of killing.

Richard Burton

Ask any striker what was the greatest goal he ever scored and they'll all give you the same answer – the next one.

Ian Rush

Foul play and cheating are the two factors that can make the game unplayable... the All Blacks are guilty of both.

Clem Thomas

The main difference between League and Union rugby is that now I get my hangovers on Monday instead of Sunday.

Tom David

Compared to the jobs I used to do, snooker is money for old rope.

Terry Griffiths

Don't ask me about emotions in the Welsh dressing room. I'm someone who cries when he watches Little House on the Prairie.

Bob Norster

... legs like tree trunks, neck muscles that put a pit bull terrier to shame, elbows flailing in the penalty box and the guts of a kamikaze bungee jumper.

Cefin Campbell on Mark Hughes

*I agree with the man
who described snooker
as chess with balls.*

Anthony Davies

*A good darts player who
can count can always beat
a brilliant one who can't.*

Leighton Rees

The reason Welsh rugby players haven't any teeth is to stop them biting each other.

Max Boyce

Love and
Marriage

My wife and I were married in a toilet: it was a marriage of convenience.

Tommy Cooper

I asked Julia Roberts for a date when we were filming Notting Hill. *I figured if she married Lyle Lovett, we all had a chance.*

Rhys Ifans

No... But he's really good at making dinner reservations.

Catherine Zeta Jones when asked if her husband could cook

*Love-making is an art
which must be studied.*

Ivor Novello

*I just don't understand when
people compare chocolate to
sex. I'm like: 'What kind of
sex are they having?' or 'What
chocolate am I eating?'*

Cerys Matthews

A national newspaper blamed the breakdown of my marriage on a blue dress I once wore!

Carol Vorderman

Welshmen haven't kissed their wives for years, but will thump anyone else who tries to do it.

Emyr Lloyd

There is no Welsh word for orgasm, but I know a very good one for adulterer.

Mair Griffiths

Eating and Drinking

*Martinis before lunch
are like a woman's
breasts. One is too few
and three are too many.*

John Humphrys

My advice if you insist on slimming: eat as much as you like – just don't swallow it.

Harry Secombe

Three things give us hardy strength: sleeping on hairy mattresses, breathing cold air, and eating dry food.

Welsh proverb

I like to drink to suit my location.

Tom Jones

*An alcoholic is someone
you don't like who drinks
as much as you do.*

Dylan Thomas

The first time I saw myself on television I was so embarrassed I stopped eating for a week.

Terry Griffiths

He could coax a meal from a brick wall if the mortar was soft enough.

Gwyn Thomas on W. H. Davies

Seeing The Lost Weekend
made me teetotal – for
two whole days.

Harry Secombe

*Teetotallers lack the sympathy
and generosity of men that drink.*

W. H. Davies

*There were once so many
pubs in Llantrisant the
church had a cork spire.*

Gwyn Thomas

I hardly ever suffered from morning sickness when I was pregnant because I was so used to hangovers.

Caitlin Thomas

Land of My
Fathers

The Welsh are such good singers because they have no locks on their bathroom doors.

Harry Secombe

But it is my happiness to be half Welsh, and that the better half.

Richard Cobden

There is a certain darkness, a lyrical darkness, in the Welsh character and that is very good for creating art.

Rob Brydon

We called the place the Welsh Embassy because there was usually somebody staying in our third bedroom.

Rhys Ifans on his childhood home

I must be the luckiest man in the world. Not only am I bisexual, I am also Welsh.

John Osbourne

Welshmen are as cunning as buggery and obvious as the day.

Caitlin Thomas

Swansea has got as many layers as an onion, and each one reduces you to tears.

Dylan Thomas

Wales isn't so much a country as a state of mind.

Ifor Williams

There is something in our weather that is hostile to treats, feasts and outings.

Gwyn Thomas

The Welsh are not meant to go out in the sun. They start to photosynthesise.

Rhys Ifans

Losing my Welsh temper meant gaining my Welsh accent.

Emlyn Williams

Down to Earth

You may be a big shot up in London, but down here in Pontypridd you wipe your shoes when you come in and take your turn bringing in the coal.

Tom Jones' mother, her first words to
Tom after he became famous

*It takes forty dumb animals
to make a fur coat but
only one to wear it.*

Bryn Jones

*It's not easy to swordfight
when you're wearing a
corset and petticoats.*

Catherine Zeta Jones

My family keeps me grounded by making me do housework.

Charlotte Church

I'd like to think I would put a coat down in a puddle for a lady. Depends on how much I paid for it, I guess.

Ioan Gruffudd

*I would have played
soccer for nothing.*

William John Charles

*Being a millionaire is a lot
like being poor, except that
you have a lot of money.*

Griff Rhys Jones

A real Welshman will admire Miss World for her politics.

Gren Jones

The Big Sleep

[He] was found on the floor of his van covered in hundreds and thousands. The police say he topped himself.

Tommy Cooper on the death of an ice cream seller

At last God caught his eye.

Harry Secombe's suggested epitaph for a bartender

Due to industrial go-slow difficulties, grave-digging this week will be done by a skeleton crew.

Sign in a Welsh cemetery

I once attended a funeral on the day Wales lost an important match against England. It totally spoiled the day for me.

Dai Jenkins

Here lies Harry Secombe until further notice.

Harry Secombe's suggestion for his headstone

My wife told me I'd drive her to the grave. I had the car out in two minutes.

Tommy Cooper

A person with no bee in their bonnet is a person in the grave.

Rhys Davies

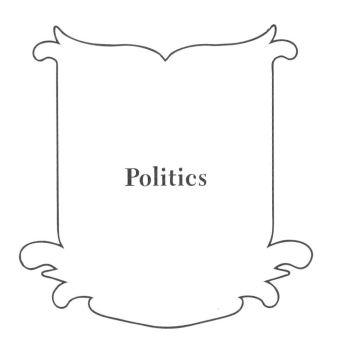

Politics

If you paint a donkey red, it will be elected in the valleys.

Welsh proverb

*The Prime Minister has
an absolute genius for
putting flamboyant labels
on empty luggage.*

Aneurin Bevan

*I warn you not to be ordinary,
I warn you not to be young, I
warn you not to fall ill, and I
warn you not to grow old.*

Neil Kinnock on the prospect of a Conservative re-election

As long as there is food and drink and greyhounds and cinemas, the majority of our people do not care what government is in power.

R. S. Thomas

I can still remember the day when I encountered my first Conservative, a shock all the greater in that it coincided with the crisis of puberty.

Gwyn Williams

This island is almost made of coal and surrounded by fish. Only an organising genius could produce a shortage of coal and fish in Great Britain at the same time.

Aneurin Bevan

Stuff and

Nonsense

*I have a face that looks
like an unmade bed.*

Dylan Thomas

When I was young I was able to hypnotise people by pulling their ear lobes.

Anthony Hopkins

Is there chicken in chick peas?

Helen Adams

There's nothing quite like
the look of a wet cat.

Lucy York

Somebody's boring me.
I think it's me.

Dylan Thomas

I'm a virgin and I brought up
all my children to be the same.

Shirley Bassey

My bottom is so big it has its own gravitational field.

Carol Vorderman

How could I have an IQ of 25 when I'm only 23?

Helen Adams

71

Idolatry is really not good for anyone. Not even the idols.

John Bach

Cats to me are strange,
so strange I cannot
sleep if one is near.

W. H. Davies

I've got nothing against
pornography except all
the bad knickers.

Cerys Matthews

I slept like a log last night;
I woke up in the fireplace.

Tommy Cooper

The Arts

The Welsh are all actors.
It's only the bad ones who
become professional.

Richard Burton

There is only one position for an artist anywhere; and that is upright.

Dylan Thomas

The only reason we wore sunglasses onstage was because we couldn't stand the sight of the audience.

John Cale

There's something cool about being a vain egotistical actor.

Ioan Gruffudd

Writers spend three years rearranging 26 letters of the alphabet. It's enough to make you lose your mind day by day.

Richard Price

One often forms a mental image of an artist through his work and is often disappointed on meeting him.

Alun Hoddinott

I've never been interested in classical music, to be honest. I'll wait until I'm deaf to get into that.

Cerys Matthews

Books write authors
as much as authors
write books.

Dick Francis

Old Age

I'll keep swivelling my hips until they need replacing.

Tom Jones

There's a deep anarchy
in old age.

Terry Jones

I'm the wrinklies'
favourite these days.

Ryan Giggs at 28

You don't get older,
you get better.

Shirley Bassey

Today I am constantly
forgetting what happened
yesterday but things that
happened 70 or 80 years ago
are becoming much clearer.

Aelwyn Roberts

Old Age

*When I go home nowadays
I get the sort of kindliness
reserved for dead people.*

Neil Kinnock

*... not by inspecting their teeth
but rather how loudly they
slam the front door shut.*

Dannie Abse on how to tell someone's age

Whatever a man does after the age of forty should be forgiven because in nine cases out of ten he is utterly worn out by what has gone on before.

Gwyn Thomas

Wise Words

You can't fashion a wit
out of two half wits.

Neil Kinnock

Things which do not require
effort of some sort are
seldom worth having.

Ivor Novello

Blame someone else and
get on with your life.

Alan Woods

A spoon does not know the taste of soup, nor a learned fool the taste of wisdom.

Welsh proverb

We know what happens to people who stay in the middle of the road. They get run over.

Aneurin Bevan

There is no point in asking a man a question until you have established whether he has any reason to lie to you.

Ken Follett

*The most dangerous
thing in the world is
to try to leap a chasm
in two jumps.*

David Lloyd George

A kleptomaniac is a person who helps himself because he can't help himself.

Henry Morgan

Man's mind is a watch that needs winding daily.

Welsh proverb

*Bad news goes about in clogs,
good news in stockinged feet.*

Welsh proverb

*The only thing we guard
with real success are the
secrets of our shames.*

Gwyn Thomas

It's easier to quote someone than to think for oneself. You can quote me on that.

Dannie Abse

www.summersdale.com